W9-ACK-192

Celebrating Virtually

Together We Can: Pandemic

By Shannon Stocker

21st Century
Junior Library

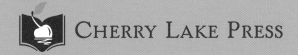

CHERRY LAKE PRESS

Published in the United States of America by Cherry Lake Publishing Group
Ann Arbor, Michigan
www.cherrylakepublishing.com

Reading Adviser: Marla Conn, MS, Ed., Literacy specialist, Read-Ability, Inc.
Photo Credits: © Aleksandra Suzi/Shutterstock.com, cover, 1; © Everett Collection/Shutterstock.com, 4;
   © Gorodenkoff/Shutterstock.com, 6; © Anna Kraynova/Shutterstock.com, 8; © New Africa/Shutterstock.com, 10;
   © Arina P Habich/Shutterstock.com, 12; © Kolpakova Daria/Shutterstock.com, 14; © Picchio Wasi/
   Shutterstock.com, 16; © Ulza/Shutterstock.com, 18; © Ivi Lichi/Shutterstock.com, 20

Cherry Lake Press is an imprint of Cherry Lake Publishing Group.

Library of Congress Cataloging-in-Publication Data

Names: Stocker, Shannon, author.
Title: Celebrating virtually / Shannon Stocker.
Description: Ann Arbor, Michigan : Cherry Lake Publishing, 2021. | Series: Together we can: pandemic | Includes
   index. | Audience: Grades 2-3 | Summary: "The COVID-19 pandemic introduced many changes into children's
   lives. Celebrating Virtually gives actionable suggestions to help young readers adapt and learn to celebrate big
   moments in new ways as we navigate the current outbreak. This book includes science content, based on current
   CDC recommendations, as well as social emotional content to help with personal wellness and development of
   empathy. All books in the 21st Century Junior Library encourage readers to think critically and creatively, and use
   their problem-solving skills. Book includes table of contents, sidebars, glossary, index, and author biography"—
   Provided by publisher.
Identifiers: LCCN 2020039997 (print) | LCCN 2020039998 (ebook) | ISBN 9781534180116 (hardcover) |
   ISBN 9781534181823 (paperback) | ISBN 9781534181120 (pdf) | ISBN 9781534182837 (ebook)
Subjects: LCSH: Internet—Social aspects—Juvenile literature. | Telecommunication—Social aspects—Juvenile literature.
Classification: LCC HM851 .S758 2021 (print) | LCC HM851 (ebook) | DDC 302.23/1—dc23
LC record available at https://lccn.loc.gov/2020039997
LC ebook record available at https://lccn.loc.gov/2020039998

Cherry Lake Publishing Group would like to acknowledge the work of the Partnership for 21st Century Learning, a
Network of Battelle for Kids. Please visit http://www.battelleforkids.org/networks/p21 for more information.

Printed in the United States of America
Corporate Graphics

CONTENTS

Life looked a lot different during the pandemic of 1918.
What differences do you see here? What similarities are there?

Why Celebrate Virtually?

Until 2020, the last time a **pandemic** hit was over 100 years ago. Then, the **coronavirus** arrived. Can you imagine what it must have been like to be **quarantined** long ago? There was no internet, no texting, no cell phones. Many people didn't even have cars! Today, we have so many different ways of staying in touch. Celebrating with friends and family doesn't have to stop just because you're quarantined.

Make and deliver cupcakes to friends before a virtual birthday party so everyone can enjoy them together.

Being quarantined can make everyone feel sad at times. It's hard to stay away from family and friends for weeks on end. **Virtual** celebrations make us feel remembered and loved. They remind us that although we might feel lonely, we are not alone.

Think!

Do you know any good jokes? Share them with a loved one today!

YouTube offers lots of how-to **tutorials**. Learn to draw or paint while video chatting!

A virtual celebration can be so much more than just a phone call or a video chat. You can still have cake, songs, gifts, themes, and, most importantly, visits from friends and family members. Be creative! Get involved in the planning! Exercising your creativity improves brain function, mental health, and physical health.

Check with your parents or teachers to find out
what platform will work best for you!

How to Celebrate Virtually

There are many different **platforms** you can use to celebrate with friends and family. If you don't have a computer, you can always call friends on the phone! But if you have a smartphone or a computer, you have choices, like FaceTime and Zoom. Be sure to do a practice session first. That way, there won't be any disappointments on the big day.

Make your own themed cake toppers.

Do you like mermaids? Video games? Horses? Pick a theme that's special to you (or whomever you're throwing the party for!) and help decorate your home. You can order supplies **online**, make your own decorations, or even print out pictures and tape them to your windows.

Create!

How many different ways can you make a party hat?
What about a centerpiece?

Drop off materials so everyone can make the same craft!

Schedule specific activities for your online party, just like you would for an in-person party. Do you want to play charades, Freeze Dance, or Simon Says? Maybe have a treasure hunt! Make your choices ahead of time so the party runs smoothly.

Start your party off by thanking your guests! Do they all know each other? If not, then let everyone introduce themselves and say something fun that they like to do. After that, it's time to start the activity!

You can mail or email a gift—or, if you live nearby,
drop it off at their front door!

Gifting during a Pandemic

Any shop that you can walk into probably has an online store. Ordering gifts from your favorite stores has never been easier. But few gifts are more treasured than those that are homemade. Draw a picture or make a craft from bits of nature. Or write a letter to tell them you love them. What better way to celebrate than with a piece of your heart?

Make a photo album of memories you've shared for a friend.

Consider creating a video **montage** through free online platforms like Tribute. Ask friends and family members to contribute photos or short videos, which they can **upload** directly to the website. Tribute will collect them, put them together, and send the montage to the person you are celebrating!

Look!

Do you have a friend or family member who has been sad? Think about making them a card or a treat that you can send to make them smile.

The best thing about a virtual party is that it doesn't matter where you live—everyone can join the fun online!

E-cards are a great way to send virtual love to people. They can come from just you or from a big group. You can send an e-card to tell someone happy birthday, get well, or good luck with the beginning of school. You can wish them happy holidays or just say hello! In fact, you never need a reason to celebrate virtually. So plan something fun today!

GLOSSARY

coronavirus (kuh-ROH-nuh-vye-ruhs) a family of viruses that cause a variety of illnesses in people and other mammals

montage (mohn-TAHJ) a video that pieces together photos or shorter videos, often put to music

online (awn-LINE) connected to another computer or network

pandemic (pan-DEM-ik) an outbreak of a disease that affects a large part of the population

platforms (PLAT-formz) electronic systems

quarantined (KWOR-uhn-teend) isolated from others

tutorials (too-TOR-ee-uhlz) instructional lessons that teach by example

upload (UHP-lohd) to transfer something from one device, like a computer, to another, often through the internet

virtual (VUR-choo-uhl) accessed by a computer, especially online

FIND OUT MORE

WEBSITES

Eventbrite—Virtual Paint Party
https://www.eventbrite.com/d/online/virtual-paint-party/?mode=search&q=virtual%20paint%20party&page=1&utm_medium=google

Paper Trail Design—Free Printable Birthday Crown
https://www.papertraildesign.com/free-printable-happy-birthday-crown

Virtual Bingo Games—Host Your Own Custom Bingo Game
https://www.bingomaker.com/web-app/?utm_medium=google

YouTube—Art for Kids Hub
https://www.youtube.com/user/ArtforKidsHub

INDEX

ABOUT THE AUTHOR

Shannon Stocker writes picture books, books for young readers, and *Chicken Soup* stories. Her virtual celebrations have included lots of Zoom calls, drawing games, and even an online painting session. Shannon lives in Louisville, Kentucky, with Greg, Cassidy, Tye, and far too many critters.